Remember the Ladies

100 GREAT AMERICAN WOMEN

CHERYL HARNESS

SCHOLASTIC INC.

New York Toronto London Auckland Sydney
Mexico City New Delhi Hong Kong Buenos Aires

ISBN 0-439-36426-4

Copyright © 2001 by Cheryl Harness.
Cover illustrations and calligraphy copyright © 2001 by Cheryl Harness.
Cover copyright © 2001 by HarperCollins Publishers.
All rights reserved.
Published by Scholastic Inc., 555 Broadway, New York, NY 10012,
by arrangement with HarperCollins Publishers.
SCHOLASTIC and associated logos are trademarks and/or registered
trademarks of Scholastic Inc.

12 11 10 9 8 7 6 5 4 3 2   2 3 4 5 6 7/0

Printed in the U.S.A.   14

First Scholastic printing, March 2002

Cover design by Stephanie Bart-Horvath

In memory of my mom, Elaine, and her mom, Eula, and her mom, Emma, and her mom, Susan, and her mom, a woman among the millions whose names are lost to us . . . —and to my legions of friends and nieces

COLUMBIA

"We hold these truths to be self-evident:
that all men and women are created equal."

Declaration of Sentiments
Elizabeth Cady Stanton, July 1848
Seneca Falls, New York

*I*n the early days of the nation, a heroic female called Columbia symbolized our country. A bronze statue of Columbia crowned with feathers and stars stands atop the Capitol dome in Washington, D.C. She represents Freedom. A majestic woman made of copper, the Statue of Liberty, holds an illuminated torch and greets voyagers to America at New York City. Newcomers might think that the United States is a nation that highly esteems her mothers, sisters, and daughters.

Well, yes and no. Men might have worshiped the ideal of woman as though she were a goddess, but, as Carrie Chapman Catt said early in the twentieth century, they "governed her as though she were an idiot." Had women been able to go to college? Own property? Work in whatever profession they wanted? Vote? Mostly, no.

Much of the story of the United States of America has been that of its Founding Fathers, Sons of Liberty, boys in uniform—its fighting, working, and governing men. The purpose of this book is to tell about 100 among millions of women who shaped our country and to, in the words of Abigail Adams, "Remember the Ladies," who, all along, have held up half of the American sky.

$\mathcal{F}$rom the point of view of 15ᵗʰ-century Europeans, North America was part of a vast *new* world. But to the million or more Indians already living there, it was as it had always been. Deep in the forests and grasslands and along the rivers, women and girls looked after the needs of their families, just as always. Their old world was about to change forever.

1542

PACIFIC OCEAN

2. POCAHONTAS

Pocahontas was also known as Matoaka (1595?–1617). Daughter of Chief Powhatan, she's said to have saved the life of Capt. John Smith in Jamestown. She married John Rolfe, who took her to England.

1692 Twenty women and girls were executed as witches at SALEM·
BOSTON·
PLYMOUTH
1620

3. PRISCILLA MULLINS ALDEN

Priscilla Mullins Alden (1602?–1685?) is remembered in Henry Wadsworth Longfellow's poem *The Courtship of Miles Standish*. Along with 74 men, she and 27 other women and girls sailed on the *Mayflower* in 1620 to Plymouth.

1607 First permanent English colony
JAMESTOWN
ROANOKE ISLAND

1. VIRGINIA DARE

Virginia Dare (1587–?) was the first English child born in America, shortly before she and the other 91 colonists disappeared forever from Roanoke Island's "Lost Colony."

·ST. AUGUSTINE
1565 First permanent European colony

1492

ATLANTIC OCEAN

4. ANNE BRADSTREET

Besides being the mother of eight children, **Anne Dudley Bradstreet** (1612?–1672) of Boston was the first important American poet.

AHOKIA

*P*eople from all over Europe, but mostly from England, came to America. Port cities bustled with ships as business prospered and the population grew, to nearly 3 million by 1775, including 500,000 African slaves.

Children learned their letters and numbers at home, in public schools, or in private "dame" schools run by women in their parlors. Higher education was only for boys. Girls were to learn the many skills needed to keep their husbands' houses running smoothly. They had no say in public life. But there were some hungry-minded girls who were given the chance to learn and express their ideas.

5. PHILLIS WHEATLEY

Mercy Otis Warren (1728–1814) of Massachusetts learned from her brothers' tutors. She wrote poetry, plays, and a three-volume history of the remarkable times she lived in—the American Revolution.

6. MERCY OTIS WARREN

One such child was sold to the Wheatley family of Boston. They taught her to read and write her new language. By the time she was twenty, **Phillis Wheatley** (1753?–1784) had published a book of poetry. She was the first African-American to be published.

For years, Americans had grumbled about the treatment they got from their Mother Country, England. Finally, in 1774, colonial delegates—all men—gathered to discuss the worsening situation. One of them, John Adams, wrote about the talks, the first battles, the Declaration of Independence, then the long war to his wife back home in Massachusetts, **Abigail Adams** (1744–1818).

Abigail hated that she'd had no formal education, but her letters to John show how much she'd read, and what wise attention she paid to their farm and children, as well as to politics and ideas. Maybe the wife of a future president and the mother of another was only teasing when she wrote about their new government:

7. ABIGAIL ADAMS

"**Remember the Ladies, and be more generous . . . to them than your ancestors. If . . . care is not paid . . . we are determined to foment a Rebelion, and will not hold ourselves bound by any Laws in which we have no voice or Representation.**"

—March 31, 1776

8. BETSY ROSS

*A*new nation needed a flag, so it's said that, in 1776, General Washington and other Continental Congressmen went to Widow Ross's upholstery shop. **Betsy Ross** (1752–1836) helped design, then sewed a banner of red (for courage), white (for purity), and blue (for justice). On June 14, 1777, the Congress officially called for a flag with 13 stars and stripes for the 13 colonies.

During the Revolutionary War, many women and their families followed their men-in-arms as nurses, cooks, and laundresses—and some became heroes. When word came that the redcoats were attacking in Connecticut, sixteen-year-old **Sybil Ludington** (1761–1839) rode her horse nearly 40 miles through the night, spreading the alarm.

9. SYBIL LUDINGTON

Margaret Corbin (1751–1800) saw her husband killed in battle in 1776. She raced to his cannon and blasted away until she herself was wounded.

Mary Hays was carrying water to the patriots fighting in June 1778, when her husband fainted from the heat. Mary, known as Molly Pitcher, took his place at his gun.

11. DEBORAH SAMPSON

One young soldier called Robert Shurtleff fought in battles. When hurt, he tended the wounds himself so that the doctors wouldn't find out "he" was really former schoolteacher **Deborah Sampson** (1760–1827). But she got sick, discovered, and discharged—a veteran of the Revolutionary War.

After the war was over, pioneers poured through the Cumberland Gap, along the National Road and Erie Canal, over the mountains, into the West and the new century. In 1804, Thomas Jefferson sent a Corps of Discovery across the continent to the Pacific. Captains Lewis and Clark were guided by their translator, a young Shoshone mother, **Sacagawea** (1786?-1812).

12. SACAGAWEA

Thousands of Americans followed **"Mother Ann" Lee** (1736–1784) into the religious group known as the Shakers. Eighteen Shaker villages dotted the young country in the Era of Good Feelings after the War of 1812.

13. ANN LEE

Emma Hart Willard (1787–1870) was a pioneer of education—the first American woman to actively campaign for higher education in math, science, and social studies for girls. She opened her first girls' school in 1814. Her Female Seminary in Troy, New York, opened in 1821, educated hundreds of teachers.

14. EMMA WILLARD

In the War of 1812, First Lady **Dolley Madison** (1768–1849) fled the President's House just before the British set fire to it in 1814. She saved important papers, the big portrait of George Washington, and her parrot. Then a summer thunderstorm saved the burning capital.

15. DOLLEY MADISON

*T*rappers and white settlers such as Eliza Spaulding and Narcissa Whitman had pushed beyond the Ohio Country into the Mississippi Valley by the 1830s. Americans thought it was the Manifest Destiny of the nation to stretch clear to the Pacific. News of gold in the West fired them up even more. They walked alongside their covered wagons on the hard four- to six-month trip on the long trails to Oregon and California. Back east, voices were being raised against slavery and for the rights of women.

OREGON COUNTRY

MINNESOTA TERRITORY

SENECA FALLS

MAINE 1820

VT 1791

NH 1788

MASS 1788

CONN 1788

R.I. 1790

WISCONSIN 1848

NY. 1788

NJ 1787

GOLD! CALIFORNIA TRAIL

UTAH TERRITORY

OREGON TRAIL

IOWA 1846

ILL. 1818

MICH. 1837

IND. 1816

OHIO 1803

PENN. 1787

MD. DEL 1788 1787

CALIFORNIA 1850

UNORGANIZED TERRITORY

W.VA. 1863

VA 1788

NEW MEXICO TERRITORY

SANTA FE TRAIL

MO. 1821

ARK. 1836

KY. 1792

NC 1789

1853

TENN. 1796

SC 1788

16. SARAH GRIMKÉ

TEXAS 1845

MISS. 1817

ALA. 1819

GA 1788

free states

MEXICO

LA. 1812

border slave states

Slave states that will leave the UNION.

FLORIDA 1845

U.S. territories

The refined **Sarah Grimké** (1792–1873) and her younger sister, Angelina, of South Carolina went to northern cities to give anti-slavery (abolitionist) talks. They were among the first women to lecture in public, shocking people who thought women should be seen and not heard. The Grimké sisters linked freedom for slaves and female equality in the fight for human rights. Laws then made it possible to take women's property, even their children.

17. ABIGAIL SCOTT DUNIWAY

19. LUCRETIA MOTT

Abigail Scott Duniway (1834–1915) was seventeen when she and her family went on the Oregon Trail. Out west, she ran a school, a hat shop, and a newspaper to support her disabled husband and six children. She also campaigned to win equal justice for women and suffrage—the right to vote.

Elizabeth Cady Stanton (1815–1902), a graduate of Emma Willard's school, got a law passed in New York that allowed married women to control their own property and wages. She helped to found the National Women's Suffrage Association.

18. ELIZABETH CADY STANTON

Lucretia Mott (1793–1880) was a Quaker minister and spitfire abolitionist (her home was a stop on the Underground Railroad).

Lucretia met Elizabeth in London when men wouldn't let them attend the World Anti-Slavery Convention. They and their friends decided to do something with their fury: They organized a public meeting. More than 300 people—men and women, black and white—came to the first women's rights convention, held in Seneca Falls, New York, July 19–20, 1848.

*S*ixty-eight women and 32 men signed Mrs. Stanton's Declaration of Sentiments, which said that "all men and women are created equal," and made a radical, first-time-ever public demand for female citizens' right to vote. They'd have to wait 72 more years.

Amelia Bloomer (1818–1894) came to the 1848 meeting in Seneca Falls. She'd be one of the first women to edit her own newspaper, the *Lily*. Determined to free women from their heavy skirts and petticoats, she started wearing "Turkish pantaloons." People just laughed at Amelia's "bloomers."

20. AMELIA BLOOMER

21. DR. ELIZABETH BLACKWELL

Six months after the convention, the first woman doctor of medicine *in modern times* graduated, first in her class, from Geneva Medical College in New York. **Dr. Elizabeth Blackwell** (1821–1910), along with her sister Emily, who became a doctor, too, opened a clinic for women and children in New York City in 1857.

Stern, determined **Susan B. Anthony** (1820–1906) and her friend Elizabeth Cady Stanton spent the entire second half of the 19th century speaking, organizing, and writing to win fair treatment and suffrage for women. Miss Anthony was cruelly criticized, made fun of, and once arrested, when she voted in the election of 1872. "Susan B." became the first woman to have her face on U.S. money—a silver dollar, issued in 1979.

23. HARRIET TUBMAN

The "slavery question" was slowly tearing the country apart. **Harriet Tubman,** aka "Moses" (1820?–1913), fled to freedom in Maryland in 1849. During the next ten years, she helped nearly 300 people, including her parents, make daring escapes from slavery.

When the inevitable Civil War broke out in 1861, hardly any American's life was untouched. Women worked to save the Union in the North or served the rebellious Confederacy in the South. They took up jobs—for way less pay—the soldiers left behind.

The great preacher Sojourner Truth, who'd stung folks with her words: "Nobody ever helps me into carriages . . . and ain't I a woman?" collected supplies for black soldiers. Harriet Tubman became a nurse, a laundress, a scout, and a spy for the Union.

24. SARAH EMMA EDMONDS

Sarah Emma Edmonds (1841–1898) was the only official female veteran of the Union army. Sarah, as "Frank Thompson," enlisted and fought in several battles. Sometimes "he" spied behind Confederate lines, convincingly dressed as a woman! But it was as herself, as a nurse, that Sarah served out the last two years of the war, then published the tales of her adventures.

Belle Boyd (1844–1900), the teenage "La Belle Rebelle," was only one of many women who were daring Confederate spies. Pauline Cushman, who was made an honorary major by President Lincoln, spied for the Union.

25. BELLE BOYD

26. CLARA BARTON

Probably the best-known woman of the Civil War (besides the fictitious Scarlett O'Hara) was **Clara Barton** (1821–1912). She was one of thousands of women, like Dr. Elizabeth Blackwell, Dr. Mary Walker (the only woman to win the Congressional Medal of Honor), and "Mother" Mary Ann Bickerdyke, who cared for the multitudes of sick and wounded soldiers. Later on, in 1881, Clara Barton started the American Red Cross.

What a growing-up time it was for the nation! New citizens and inventions came into the American story. New ideas, too: In 1872, after she and her sister ran the first woman-owned stock brokerage, journalist **Victoria Woodhull** (1838–1937) ran for the Presidency of the United States.

27 VICTORIA WOODHULL

VICTORIA WOODHULL for PRESIDENT 1872

28. LOUISA MAY ALCOTT

From 1860 to 1890, 10 million European immigrants joined freed blacks and everyone else pursuing the dream and the dollar in hard, crowded cities, in offices, mines, mills, and smoking, clacking factories. One poor struggling writer, a former Civil War nurse, was writing a book about herself and her sisters. It would be a best-seller in 1868. People still love reading *Little Women*, by **Louisa May Alcott** (1832–1888).

Plenty of Civil War veterans went out to the plains to fight Indians—what was left of them: a fifth as many as when the Pilgrims landed. Paiute tribal leader and daring scout **Sarah Winnemucca** (1844?–1891) met with President

30. SARAH JOSEPHA HALE

In the 1880s, people on both sides of the Atlantic Ocean crowded to see Buffalo Bill's idea of the vanishing Wild West. One of his most popular acts was deadeye crack-shot **Annie Oakley**, born Phoebe Ann Moses (1860–1926). She could drill a dime tossed in the air.

It was full of essays, poems, and colored pictures of the latest fashions. **Sarah J. B. Hale** (1788–1879) edited—for fifty years—this most popular women's magazine of the 19th century, but she is most remembered for writing a poem, "Mary Had a Little Lamb."

29. SARAH WINNEMUCCA

32. ANNIE OAKLEY

31. EMILY DICKINSON

Hayes and talked to white audiences about the suffering of her people, but it was no use. Their world was disappearing.

One of the most legendary women of the frontier was **Calamity Jane** (1852?–1903), otherwise known as rough-talking Martha Jane Canary Burk, scout for General Custer and heroine of many a dime novel.

Trains chugged all the way to the blue Pacific, past sod houses and bleached buffalo bones. Lonely pioneer women and girls in these homesteads hoped the trains might bring a copy of *Godey's Lady's Book.*

One of the great American poets of the 19th century was not well known at all until after she died. **Emily Dickinson** (1830–1886) was just too shy. Her secret poems are still carefully studied and admired.

33. CALAMITY JANE

*I*n the 1880s and 1890s, deadly violence broke out between striking workers and their employers. Americans were proud of booming U.S. industry, but they were troubled about the human cost when they read stories by the first woman investigative reporter, Elizabeth Cochrane Seaman, aka **Nellie Bly** (1867–1922). She went undercover in factories, jails, and even an insane asylum to tell how poor people were working and living. But her most famous story was outdoing the made-up hero of Jules Verne's novel *Around the World in 80 Days*. Nellie Bly made it in 72 days, 6 hours, and 11 minutes (November 1889–January 1890).

34. NELLIE BLY

35. BELVA LOCKWOOD

Belva Lockwood (1830–1917) completed another sort of journey. In 1879, she became the first female lawyer allowed to practice her profession before the judges of the Supreme Court. The Equal Rights party nominated her as its presidential candidate in 1884 and 1888.

Millions of people had a swell time at the World's Columbian Exposition in Chicago in 1893. They rode 250 feet into the air on a new invention, the Ferris wheel.

38. CARRY NATION

They saw a mural painted by the great American Impressionist **Mary Cassatt** (1845–1926).

People admired the sculptures of Anne Whitney and the music

36. MARY CASSATT

of brilliant violinist Maud Powell. They heard the fiery Kansas orator Mary Lease, and the last lectures of suffragist **Lucy Stone** (1818–1893), the first American woman to refuse to give up her own name when she got married. Stubborn. She had to be.

37. LUCY STONE

Carry Nation (1846-1911) was every bit as stubborn when it came to drinking. She was dead set against it. So, in 1899, she started wrecking Kansas saloons with her hatchet. "Hatchetation," she called it.

Meanwhile, the 19th century came to an end with 4 million Americans riding exciting new inventions: bicycles. A war burst out with Spain, and America burst onto the world's stage.

A whole new century: Change was in the air. Americans saw much that needed fixing, but they believed all kinds of progress was possible. Look what they already had: electric light! Horseless carriages! Moving pictures! The Wright brothers had conquered the air!

With the help of her valiant teacher, Annie Sullivan, twenty-two-year-old **Helen Keller** (1880–1968) had conquered blindness and deafness, graduated with honors from Radcliffe College, and written her autobiography. She became a champion for the disabled.

39. HELEN KELLER

40. JANE ADDAMS

Jane Addams (1860–1935) and her friends began Hull House in Chicago to help the poor with day care, legal and medical help, and classes. Miss Addams, who won the Nobel Peace Prize in 1931, invented the profession of social work. She inspired a generation of young people such as Eleanor Roosevelt.

Americans adored reading about Eleanor's uncle, President Teddy Roosevelt, and his family, especially his willful daughter, Alice.

She was like a real-life Gibson Girl. Drawn by the artist Charles Dana Gibson, the Gibson Girl was the most popular—but imaginary—woman in the country.

An especially real and determined woman was labor leader **Mary Harris Jones** (1830–1930). "Mother" Jones spent her long life helping workers fight

At about this time, American dancers **Isadora Duncan** (1878–1927) and Loïe Fuller were revolutionizing the art of dance with their personal, liquid way of floating about, using light, music, and flowing costumes.

43. ISADORA DUNCAN

41. MOTHER JONES

for safer conditions and shorter hours in the textile mills and coal mines.

In 1911, **Harriet Quimby** (1875–1912) became the first American woman to get a pilot's license and

42. HARRIET QUIMBY

the first woman to fly a plane across the English Channel. She died in a crash in 1912.

They made beauty.

Beauty was also the business of Sarah B. McWilliams (1867–1919), who became known as **Madame C. J. Walker**. This laundress developed a formula for smooth, glossy hair in 1905. She sold her "Walker method"

44. MADAME C.J. WALKER

door-to-door, and became a million-aire—the first black businesswoman to do so.

45. MARY PICKFORD

Tango-dancing, Castle-walking Americans loved piling into their "Tin Lizzies" to go hear John Philip Sousa's band. They paid 5¢ at the "nickelodeons" to see silent movies starring "America's Sweetheart," **Mary Pickford** (1893–1979). She organized the United Artists Corporation with Charlie Chaplin, D. W. Griffith, and Douglas Fairbanks.

46. JULIETTE GORDON "DAISY" LOW

When girls left the theater, they could meet with their scout troop, thanks to **Juliette Gordon Low** (1860–1927). To help girls become self-reliant and independent, she started the Girl Scouts in 1912.

Margaret Sanger (1883–1966) thought that no female would ever be free and independent without control over having babies. This was such an outrageous idea that Mrs. Sanger got thrown in jail, after opening the nation's first birth-control clinic in 1916. She was like those stubborn suffragettes carrying posters in front of the White House, getting arrested for demanding the vote. They upset some people pretty badly—and gave others hope.

47. MARGARET SANGER

48. IDA BELL WELLS-BARNETT

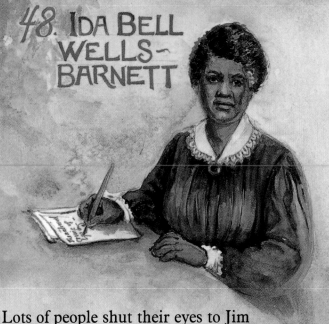

Lots of people shut their eyes to Jim Crow laws that closed opportunities to black citizens, who were still being lynched—brutally hanged. So journalist **Ida Bell Wells-Barnett** (1862–1931), known as "Iola," had to work very hard demanding justice for blacks, and votes for women, whatever color they were. She crusaded against lynching all over the country.

Americans didn't want to hear about trouble, and certainly not trouble overseas. But they couldn't help reading about the German Kaiser invading Belgium, or about Americans drowning when a German torpedo sank the ocean liner *Lusitania*. President Wilson declared war on Germany in April of 1917. American women drove ambulances and nursed soldiers shattered in the trenches. Back home, they raised money for the war. When the Great War ended in 1918, they'd make the last big push for the Vote.

49. ELIZABETH GURLEY FLYNN

Elizabeth Gurley Flynn (1890–1964), the "Rebel Girl," was a teenager when she made speeches for workers' rights and led strikes for the Industrial Workers of the World. She helped start the American Civil Liberties Union in 1920.

*T*he war had been so awful, it changed how people looked at the world—and at women, who still couldn't vote for their nation's leaders. **Alice Paul** (1885–1977) protested! She chained herself to the White House gates. In jail, she wouldn't eat— and was cruelly force-fed. What a triumph it was for Alice and **Carrie Chapman Catt** (1859–1947), the determined leader of the National American Woman Suffrage Association, and for millions of American women, when they finally won full citizenship: the right to vote. At last, on August 26, 1920, the ladies were remembered.

50. ALICE PAUL

51. CARRIE CHAPMAN CATT

MR. PRESIDENT HOW LONG MUST WOMEN WAIT FOR LIBERTY

Vote

In the Roaring Twenties, business boomed and working people were buying cars and radios—on credit, if they had to. They cheered heroes like baseball slugger Babe Ruth, pioneer aviator Charles Lindbergh, and flier Bessie Coleman, the first black female with a pilot's license.

52. ANNIE SMITH PECK

The north peak of Mount Huascarán in Peru was named after the professor who conquered it, **Annie Smith Peck** (1850–1935). No American woman in this hemisphere had climbed higher: nearly 22,000 feet.

53 GERTRUDE EDERLE

Twenty-year-old **Gertrude Ederle** (1906–) was the first woman to swim the English Channel. She swam 35 miles in 14.5 hours and came home to a ticker-tape parade in New York City.

"Flappers" started "bobbing" (cutting off) their long hair and skirts so they could look like film star **Clara Bow**, (1905–1965), the "It Girl" in the movies. They wanted to dance the Charleston to jazz music. But if they and their boyfriends wanted to drink alcohol—that was against the U.S. Constitution as of 1919. Folks went to "speakeasies," and "bootleggers" smuggled bottles of "bathtub gin" in their boot tops. Gangsters were shooting machine guns at one another in these Prohibition times.

54. CLARA BOW

Annie Jump Cannon (1863–1941) had no interest in flapping. She followed in the footsteps of astronomer Maria Mitchell. Miss Cannon, "census taker of the sky," recorded and studied thousands of stars. She received an honorary doctorate from Oxford University in 1925, a first for women.

55. ANNIE JUMP CANNON

"Black Thursday" is what people called October 24, 1929, when the stock market in New York City crashed and the Great Depression began. Banks and businesses failed. Millions were broke and out of a job, so it was a bowed-down and scared American people who elected FDR, Franklin D. Roosevelt, in 1932. It calmed them to listen on their radios to his "fireside chats" about his New Deal government programs to help people and the sick economy.

56. FRANCES PERKINS

His secretary of labor, **Frances Perkins** (1882–1965), the first woman to be a member of a presidential cabinet, helped get it going.

57. MARY McLEOD BETHUNE

Mary McLeod Bethune (1875–1955), a teacher who'd built an outstanding school in Florida, became director of the Division of Negro Affairs of the National Youth Administration: the first black woman to head a federal agency. The First Lady, Eleanor Roosevelt, a hard worker in her own right for civil rights, had championed Mrs. Bethune.

Mrs. Roosevelt also saw to it that **Marian Anderson** (1902–1993) could lift her pure voice in song at the Lincoln Memorial on Easter Sunday in 1939. Because she was black, she'd been shut out of a Washington concert hall. She went on to be the first black woman to sing at the Metropolitan Opera in New York City, in 1955.

58. MARIAN ANDERSON

59. LAURA INGALLS WILDER

60. SHIRLEY TEMPLE

The same year FDR was elected, 1932, people read the first of the "Little House" books. **Laura Ingalls Wilder** (1867–1957) wrote about her pioneer girlhood. It heartened folks going through tough times to read about the loving Ingalls family surviving on the frontier.

61. AMELIA EARHART

And it cheered them to sit in the dark and watch a smiling, curly-headed little girl tap-dancing across a silvery screen. That's why **Shirley Temple** Black (1928–) was the most popular movie star in Hollywood. She became the U.S. ambassador to Ghana and the first woman to be chief of protocol in the State Department.

Another person captured the people's imagination in the Thirties. **Amelia Earhart** (1897–1937?), the first woman to fly solo across the Atlantic Ocean, in 1932, flew even farther in 1935. She'd almost flown clear around the world when her plane was lost at sea in 1937 and never found. A mystery still.

*H*arsh leaders were in power: Stalin in the Soviet Union, Mussolini in Italy, Tojo in Japan, and Franco in Spain. Worst of all, Nazi leader Adolf Hitler had Germany and wanted the world. His tanks rolled into Poland in the fall of 1939, then blitzed across Europe in the spring of 1940. President Roosevelt led America into all-out World War II when Japan attacked the U.S. base at Pearl Harbor, Hawaii, December 7, 1941.

VICTORY GARDEN

WOMEN WAR WORKERS

62.
JACQUELINE COCHRAN

63.
ELEANOR ROOSEVELT

Millions of women worked in aircraft plants and ship-yards. One hundred thousand joined the army. Flier **Jacqueline Cochran** (1910?–1980) organized 1,000 WASPs—Women's Airforce Service Pilots. She earned the Distinguished Service Medal and, in 1953, was the first woman to fly faster than the speed of sound.

Eleanor Roosevelt (1884–1962) had long since changed from a shy young woman to the most active First Lady ever. From 1933 to 1945, she traveled all over the world for FDR, her wheelchair-bound husband. She worked hard for human rights all her life.

Folks read Mrs. Roosevelt's daily newspaper column, listened to Mary Margaret McBride on the radio, and saw Bette Davis and Katharine Hepburn movies. They admired dancers/choreographers

They admired the flowers, and bones, and bright, bleak New Mexican landscapes painted by **Georgia O'Keeffe** (1887–1986).

66. GEORGIA O'KEEFFE

64. KATHERINE DUNHAM

such as Martha Graham and **Katherine Dunham** (1910–), anthropologist and author.

65. DIDRIKSON "BABE" ZAHARIAS

People cheered women's baseball and followed the exploits of champion golfer **Babe Didrikson Zaharias** (1914–1956). She was great at every other sport, too.

Two women who had photographed folks' struggles in the Great Depression now made pictures of the war. The first woman to be an official war correspondent for the U.S. Army was **Margaret Bourke-White** (1906–1971). When U.S. tanks invaded Germany, she was there. And when the concentration camps were liberated, she was there, too. Dorothea Lange captured images of Japanese-Americans locked up in camps, in case they were spies.

67. MARGARET BOURKE-WHITE

By the fall of 1945, 55 million people were dead and atomic power had been let loose over Japan. The United Nations and the state of Israel were born, along with the Cold War between the communist USSR (aka Russia or the Soviet Union) in the East and the democratic nations in the West, led by the United States.

With the Fifties came increased fear of communism, along with an arms race and, when the USSR launched the satellite *Sputnik* in 1957, a space race. A bus boycott, led by Dr. Martin Luther King, Jr., began on a December afternoon in 1955, in Montgomery, Alabama, after the "mother of the civil rights movement," **Rosa Parks** (1913–), refused to give up her seat to a white man.

68. ROSA PARKS

The Baby Boom began when hundreds of thousands of soldiers came home from World War II. People got married and started having babies. All those babies' mommies were encouraged to stay in their new suburban homes and take care of their families while daddies worked to make money. Sometimes people needed advice about the changing times, so they started writing to a pair of sisters, then looked in the newspapers to see what Ann Landers (Esther Friedman) or Dear Abby (her twin sister, Pauline) had to say.

In homes across the land, people gathered around their flickering black-and-white video campfires.

This and other ways that people lived together, in families and tribes, were studied by anthropologist **Margaret Mead** (1901–1978).

71. MARIA TALLCHIEF

As Lucy was making people laugh, **Maria Tallchief** (1925–) was dancing. Born on an Osage Indian reservation in Oklahoma, she became a prima ballerina of the New York City Ballet and the first American ballerina to win international fame.

69. MARGARET MEAD

People watched Elvis Presley rocking and rolling on *The Ed Sullivan Show* on a Sunday night in 1956. On Monday nights, they rocked their babies and watched a show started by television pioneers **Lucille Ball** (1911–1989) and Desi Arnaz. It was so funny that millions of people around the world still watch *I Love Lucy*.

70. LUCILLE BALL

72. WILMA RUDOLPH

At seven, **Wilma Rudolph** (1940–1994) had been sick and lost the use of her leg. But she moved and worked until she could walk, then run, then become an outstanding track star. She broke world records and was the first American woman to win three gold medals at one Olympics, in 1960.

ohn F. Kennedy's time was called the New Frontier. Idealistic young Americans joined the Peace Corps to work and teach abroad. But back home, black and white Americans struggled mightily over the kind of nation they wanted. Overseas, an Iron Curtain hung across Europe: the free West on one side, communist dictatorships on the other. And running through the middle of the divided capital of Germany, the Berlin Wall symbolized the Cold War at its coldest.

73.
JACQUELINE
KENNEDY
ONASSIS

Still, the president and his young family were popular, especially his stylish wife, **Jacqueline Kennedy** (1929-1994). Jackie brought American art and artists into the White House and educated Americans about its history. She was admired greatly for her dignity when President Kennedy was assassinated in 1963.

In these days, explorers were going up in rockets to study the frontier of space. Others were going down into the ocean to study the deep frontier of the aquasphere.

One bold adventurer determined to study the plants growing under the sea was intrepid scientist, mom, and environmentalist **Sylvia Earle** (1935–). She walked untethered on the ocean floor, farther down than any other human, 1,250 feet under the surface of the sea. This daring feat earned Dr. Earle the title Her Deepness.

74. SYLVIA EARLE

In 1962, biologist **Rachel Carson** (1907–1964) wrote *Silent Spring*, a book about how plants and creatures in the vast natural world depended on one another and were being damaged by weed killer and bug spray. Her serious work encouraged the environmental movement to save the planet.

75. RACHEL CARSON

76. BETTY FRIEDAN

Generally, women were shut out from creative, professional work away from their homes. The serious—but unpaid—work of raising a family was a woman's traditional job. Young girls were playing dolls with curvy, teeny-footed Barbie and given Miss America as a swimsuited (or evening-gowned) role model.

In 1963, author **Betty Friedan** (1921–) wrote a book about the problem of females not being taken seriously and called it *The Feminine Mystique*. Her book, and Rachel Carson's, were far more than the best-sellers they were. They got people thinking and talking about how people live with one another and their environment.

What was happening in America? Changing times. The fight for justice for blacks spread out to include women and others who felt left out and left behind. The sons (and some daughters) of the Baby Boom were fighting and dying in the unpopular Vietnam War. At home, the young challenged the authority of the grown-ups with their own music and ideas, and even violence. Not long before President Kennedy was killed in 1963, Dr. Martin Luther King, Jr., had led 200,000 Freedom Marchers to Washington, D.C., and told people his dream of racial equality. When he was killed in 1968, American cities exploded in smoky riots.

Even so, there were rays of light. New civil rights laws were passed. **Shirley Chisolm** (1924–) became the first black woman to serve in the U.S. Congress in 1969. She went on to run for President in 1972.

77. SHIRLEY CHISHOLM

78. JEANNETTE RANKIN

Young and old protested the increasingly unsupportable Vietnam War. **Jeannette Rankin** (1880–1973), the first woman elected to Congress and the only person to vote against the U.S. entering both World War I and World War II, was eighty-seven years old when she led 5,000 women in an antiwar march on the U.S. Capitol.

The elderly birth control warrior Margaret Sanger lived to see a victory in her battle—a pill so a woman could choose if she would have a baby. Later on, in 1973, a *very* controversial decision was made by the Supreme Court: Abortion was allowed. These developments led to changing attitudes about how men and women got along together.

The work of **Dian Fossey** (1932–1985) led to changed notions about how people and wild animals got along together in a world with fewer and fewer wild places. Until a human killed her, she studied the friendly, intelligent mountain gorillas of Africa.

After 1969, children could go to *Sesame Street* to learn their letters and numbers, thanks to **Joan Ganz Cooney** (1929–).

79. DIAN FOSSEY

80. JOAN GANZ COONEY

81. JULIA CHILD

And after 1969, people could look up at the moon and imagine folks walking there. When people went inside, they could make something pretty good for supper, if they'd been watching jolly, brilliant chef **Julia Child** (1912–) on the French cooking show she began in 1963.

*M*s. **Gloria Steinem** (1934–)—not Miss, not Mrs.: Who needed to know if a lady was married? That was the idea!—started a new magazine, called *Ms.* It reflected the ideas and goals of the women's liberation movement: equal pay for equal work and an Equal Rights Amendment (ERA). Then the Constitution would say, as Elizabeth Cady Stanton had, "all men and women are created equal."

82. GLORIA STEINEM

83. BARBARA JORDAN

The ERA didn't become the law of the land, but still, women were getting important work done. Marian Wright Edelman started the Children's Defense Fund. People such as the powerful **Barbara Jordan** (1936–1996), the first black congresswoman to be elected from the Deep South, and Geraldine Ferraro, 1984 Democratic vice-presidential candidate, entered politics. Republican Nancy Kassebaum of Kansas made it to the U.S. Senate on her own, not as a senator's widow.

84. SARAH CALDWELL

The fight for equality was symbolized, in 1973, by a tennis match between a man, Bobby Riggs, and a woman, **Billie Jean King** (1943–).

87. BILLIE JEAN KING

For the first time, a woman, professor **Sarah Caldwell** (1928–) conducted the New York Philharmonic, then the Metropolitan Opera.

Barbara Walters (1931–) became the first woman to coanchor the network evening news. She changed the look of television. Meanwhile, **Katharine Graham** (1917–) was building the *Washington Post* into a newspaper of national importance.

85. BARBARA WALTERS

86. KATHARINE GRAHAM

Not only did she beat him—on prime-time television—she and others, such as Rosemary Casals and Chris Evert, brought money to the sport and respect for women athletes. For one thing, girls were allowed into the Little League, in 1974.

Another contest was going on between the President and the people. In the pages of the *Washington Post* were stories about scheming in the White house and a burglary at the Watergate building. In the end, in 1974, Richard Nixon, the first president to go to China, became the first to give up his job—because the stories were true. It cast a long shadow over the nation's 200th birthday.

People watched their changing culture reflected on MTV, designed by Judy McGrath, or went to movies directed by Penny Marshall. In quieter moments, Americans thought about freedom's complicated cost as they traced their fingers over the 58,000 names of dead soldiers inscribed in the polished black granite walls of the memorial dedicated in 1982 to the veterans of the Vietnam War. It was designed by a twenty-one-year-old student of architecture, **Maya Ying Lin** (1959–).

88. MAYA YING LIN

89. GRACE HOPPER

In 1981, President Reagan appointed the first woman to be one of the nine justices of the U.S. Supreme Court: **Sandra Day O'Connor** (1930–). Ruth Bader Ginsburg joined her there in 1993.

Folks faxed each other about life-changing computers pioneered by math genius and cyber-language inventor **Grace Hopper**, Ph.D. (1906–1992). "Amazing Grace" was a rear admiral in the U.S. Navy, the first woman to achieve that rank.

90. SANDRA DAY O'CONNOR

The first Hispanic woman to be surgeon general was doctor **Antonia Novello** (1944–). This pediatrician and native of Puerto Rico became the nation's top doctor.

91.
ANTONIA
NOVELLO

People in the 1980s were frightened of the AIDS epidemic and international terrorism. The Cold War and communist control of Eastern Europe were coming to an end. Eastern Europeans were protesting their communist governments.

Meanwhile, high above the blue planet crowded with bombers and hostage takers, disco dancers, recyclers, and joggers, the first American woman sped through space: Dr. **Sally Ride** (1951–).

92.
SALLY
RIDE

NASA

She'd be followed by others: teacher Christa McAuliffe, Mae Jemison, Ellen Ochoa, Shannon Lucid, and Eileen Collins, the first woman to command and pilot a spacecraft.

While they studied outer space, **Oprah Winfrey** (1954–) studied a kind of inner space: what people were thinking and feeling. This actress, communicator, studio owner, and film producer started her national talk show in 1986.

93.
OPRAH
WINFREY

Martha Stewart (1941–) takes care of another sort of inner space: inside people's homes and kitchens. Outside, too, in their gardens. A lot of "good things" are in her books, magazines, and newspaper column and on her television show for people who want to do things better—like tireless Martha, domestic empress.

94.
MARTHA
STEWART

Out of a collection of colonies came a revolutionary nation based on the idea that a free people should be able to govern themselves. Were all the people to be free and equal? Could boys and girls grow up together, standing on their own sturdy feet as full, thoughtful citizens? The world's gone around the sun many a time with those questions still being answered.

Still, imagine Virginia Dare's mother or Priscilla Alden and the Pilgrims being told that the U.S. had become a gigantic, powerful nation. Could Sarah Grimké have imagined Oprah Winfrey and Rosie O'Donnell talking to millions of people every day? If only Belva Lockwood could know that two women are Supreme Court judges. And imagine the wonder of Harriet Quimby and Amelia Earhart, knowing how fast and far Jacqueline Cochran and Sally Ride were able to fly!

Could Phillis Wheatley have imagined that a proud, wise black woman, a former cable-car conductor and actress, would one day read her own poetry for the inauguration of a president? But author **Maya Angelou** (1928–) did just that, in 1993. Emily Dickinson would shiver with shyness!

**96.
MADELEINE ALBRIGHT**

UNITED STATES

**95.
MAYA ANGELOU**

Wouldn't Elizabeth Cady Stanton and Susan B. Anthony smile proudly over their teacups, knowing that a woman is the nation's chief diplomat, representing their country in the community of nations? But that is the role of **Madeleine Albright** (1937–), the first woman to become U.S. secretary of state.

Could Sacagawea have imagined the vast continent, and beyond, crisscrossed with highways? Settled up with 250 million citizens of the United States? And the native peoples on poor reservations? Maybe it would have encouraged struggling Louisa May Alcott and Ida Bell Wells-Barnett to know that **Toni Morrison** (1931–), writer of soaring words, would win the Nobel Prize for literature, the first black American woman to do so.

99.
JULIE TAYMOR

97.
TONI
MORRISON

Jane Addams would nod with satisfaction at the work done by fellow Nobel Peace Prize–winner **Jody Williams** (1950–). Her mission is an international campaign to ban land mines: little buried bombs that cripple and kill.

Imagine Mary Pickford, Katherine Dunham, and Isadora Duncan sitting in a dark theater watching the amazing dancing puppetry designed by **Julie Taymor** (1952–).

100.
RUTH J. SIMMONS

98.
JODY
WILLIAMS

Imagine the pride of Emma Willard and Harriet Tubman if they could know that **Ruth J. Simmons** (1945–), a great-great-granddaughter of slaves, presides over nearly 3,000 women of all colors studying together at Smith College—the first black woman to hold such a position.

*I*magine Abigail Adams gazing into a glowing monitor, tapping a keyboard with slender fingers, writing a letter to her beloved John or her friend Mercy Otis Warren about their country in the 21st century. She'd be boggled by speed and noise, by the bigness of the nation and its government. She'd be shocked at the violence and disrespect in public schools where boys and girls can be freely educated. She'd glory in the freedom and achievement of American women in business, the arts, education, science, sports, and government. Then she'd "Remember the Ladies" who made it all possible, who are making possible what remains to be achieved. IMAGINE!

To Help You "Remember the Ladies"

1. Virginia Dare, colonist
2. Pocahontas, Native American
3. Priscilla Mullins Alden, Pilgrim
4. Anne Dudley Bradstreet, poet
5. Phillis Wheatley, poet
6. Mercy Otis Warren, playwright, historian
7. Abigail Adams, observer, correspondent, patriot, First Lady
8. Betsy Ross, patriot, seamstress
9. Sybil Ludington, Revolutionary War hero
10. Margaret Corbin, Revolutionary War hero
11. Deborah Sampson, soldier
12. Sacagawea, guide, translator
13. "Mother Ann" Lee, religious leader
14. Emma Hart Willard, educator
15. Dolley Madison, First Lady, social leader
16. Sarah Grimké, abolitionist, suffragist
17. Abigail Scott Duniway, pioneer, suffragist, journalist
18. Elizabeth Cady Stanton, suffragist, author, organizer
19. Lucretia Mott, abolitionist
20. Amelia Bloomer, journalist, dress reformer
21. Elizabeth Blackwell, doctor
22. Susan B. Anthony, suffragist, author
23. Harriet Tubman, emancipator, Union scout
24. Sarah Emma Edmonds, soldier
25. Belle Boyd, Confederate spy
26. Clara Barton, nurse, Red Cross founder
27. Victoria Woodhull, journalist, presidential candidate
28. Louisa May Alcott, author
29. Sarah Winnemucca, author, teacher
30. Sarah J. B. Hale, author, editor, poet
31. Emily Dickinson, poet
32. Annie Oakley, markswoman, performer
33. Calamity Jane, scout
34. Nellie Bly, reporter, adventurer
35. Belva Lockwood, teacher, lawyer
36. Mary Cassatt, painter
37. Lucy Stone, social reformer
38. Carry Nation, temperance campaigner
39. Helen Keller, author, lecturer
40. Jane Addams, social worker
41. Mary Harris Jones, labor activist
42. Harriet Quimby, journalist, aviator
43. Isadora Duncan, dancer
44. Madame C. J. Walker, entrepreneur, inventor
45. Mary Pickford, actress, businesswoman
46. Juliette Gordon Low, youth leader
47. Margaret Sanger, birth-control pioneer

48. Ida Bell Wells-Barnett, social reformer, journalist
49. Elizabeth Gurley Flynn, labor activist
50. Alice Paul, suffragist, founder National Woman's Party
51. Carrie Chapman Catt, suffragist, reformer
52. Annie Smith Peck, mountain climber, professor
53. Gertrude Ederle, swimmer
54. Clara Bow, actress
55. Annie Jump Cannon, astronomer
56. Frances Perkins, government official
57. Mary McLeod Bethune, educator
58. Marian Anderson, singer
59. Laura Ingalls Wilder, pioneer, author
60. Shirley Temple, actress, diplomat
61. Amelia Earhart, aviator
62. Jacqueline Cochran, aviator, businesswoman
63. Eleanor Roosevelt, First Lady, humanitarian
64. Katherine Dunham, choreographer, anthropologist
65. Babe Didrikson Zaharias, athlete
66. Georgia O'Keeffe, painter
67. Margaret Bourke-White, photographer
68. Rosa Parks, civil rights figure
69. Margaret Mead, anthropologist
70. Lucille Ball, comedienne
71. Maria Tallchief, ballerina
72. Wilma Rudolph, athlete
73. Jacqueline Kennedy (Onassis), First Lady, editor
74. Sylvia Earle, marine botanist
75. Rachel Carson, author, biologist
76. Betty Friedan, author, activist
77. Shirley Chisolm, congresswoman
78. Jeannette Rankin, congresswoman, peace activist
79. Dian Fossey, observer of animal behavior
80. Joan Ganz Cooney, children's television pioneer
81. Julia Child, chef, author
82. Gloria Steinem, author, activist
83. Barbara Jordan, congresswoman
84. Sarah Caldwell, opera conductor
85. Barbara Walters, broadcaster, journalist
86. Katharine Graham, newspaper publisher
87. Billie Jean King, athlete
88. Maya Ying Lin, architect
89. Rear Adm. Grace Hopper, computer pioneer
90. Sandra Day O'Connor, Supreme Court justice
91. Antonia Novello, surgeon general
92. Sally Ride, astronaut
93. Oprah Winfrey, communicator, actress
94. Martha Stewart, businesswoman
95. Maya Angelou, author
96. Madeleine Albright, diplomat
97. Toni Morrison, author
98. Jody Williams, peace activist
99. Julie Taymor, theatrical designer
100. Ruth J. Simmons, educator

Glossary

Abolitionist someone who wanted to abolish (end) slavery before the Civil War

AIDS (Acquired Immune Deficiency Syndrome): a contagious virus carried in the bloodstream that has resulted in a deadly worldwide epidemic

Ambassador a high-ranking diplomat, one who represents a nation in its dealings with other nations. The formal, proper manners used by diplomats are called *protocol*.

Anthropologist one who studies the ways and beliefs of people

Atomic power the energy that is released when there are changes at the core (nucleus) of an atom

Boycott when people, to make a point, join together, refusing to buy or sell or use something

Castle-walking a dance made popular by Vernon and Irene Castle

Communism the idea that property should be owned by a whole community. For many years after 1917, Russia's government was communist. Russia and the countries nearby were controlled so sternly, it was as if they were locked behind an *Iron Curtain*. From 1946 to the early 1990s, the tense relationship between Russia and the U.S. was called the *Cold War*. One result of it was a *Wall* across Berlin to keep those in the communist part of that city from escaping. Another was the *Vietnam War* (1957–1975), meant to keep that part of Southeast Asia from being communist. It didn't work.

Concentration camps where millions of people, unwanted by Adolf Hitler, were sent to work and die

Confederacy the government formed by the 11 states that left the Union of the U.S., 1860–1861

Cyber-language how one talks to computers and how they compute and talk to each other

Dictatorship a government controlled by a person with absolute power

Freedom Marchers people walking together to express anger and desire for change

Horseless carriage automobile. Henry Ford's Model T was also called a **Tin Lizzie**.

Insane asylum where people suffering with mental illness used to be sent

Jim Crow the slang way to refer to laws and customs that discriminated against black people

Manifest Destiny the belief Americans had in the early 19th century that the U.S. should spread out across the continent "from sea to shining sea"

New Deal Franklin Roosevelt's ideas for helping the country through the hard times of the 1930s

Nobel Prize established in 1901 by Alfred Nobel, the inventor of dynamite, to honor great thinkers

Prohibition the period, 1919–1933, when the 18th Amendment made selling alcohol illegal in the U.S. Some people would go to secret places called **speakeasies** and drink anyway.

Redcoats what red-uniformed British soldiers were called in the American Revolution

Satellite a small moon, natural or manmade, revolving around a planet

Smallpox a virus that used to kill people all over the world until a vaccine was developed

Stock brokerage where people go to invest in companies

Suffragist someone who works for people's civil right to vote. Women were sometimes called **suffragettes**.

Supreme Court the highest court in the nation

Bibliography

Butterfield, L. H., Marc Friedlander, and Mary Jo Kline, eds. *The Book of Abigail and John: Selected Letters of the Adams Family 1762–1784*. Cambridge, Mass.: Harvard University Press, 1975.

Butterfield, Roger. *The American Past*. New York: Simon & Schuster, 1947.

Colman, Penny. *Spies! Women in the Civil War*. Cincinnati, Oh.: Betterway, 1992.

Glennon, Lorraine, ed. *Our Times: Illustrated History of the 20th Century*. Atlanta: Turner, 1995.

Greenspan, Karen. *The Timetables of Women's History*. New York: Simon & Schuster, 1994.

Grun, Bernard. *The Timetables of History*. New York: Simon & Schuster, 1982.

Lunardini, Christine. *What Every American Should Know About Women's History*. Holbrook, Mass.: Adams Media, 1997.

McHenry, Robert, ed. *Famous American Women*. New York: Dover, 1983.

Ward, Geoffrey C., and Ken Burns. *Not for Ourselves Alone*. New York: Knopf, 1999.

Wirth, Conrad L., et al. *America's Historylands*. Washington D.C.: National Geographic Society, 1962.

The World Book Encyclopedia. Chicago: World Book.

Recommended Reading

If you want to read more, here are a few suggestions to get you started.

Blos, Joan W. *Nellie Bly's Monkey*. New York: Morrow, 1996.

Bober, Natalie S. *Abigail Adams, Witness to a Revolution*. New York: Atheneum, 1995.

Clarke, Mary Stetson. *Bloomers and Ballots*. New York: Viking, 1972.

Clinton, Susan. *The Story of Susan B. Anthony*. Chicago: Children's Press, 1986.

Clyne, Patricia Edwards. *Patriots in Petticoats*. New York: Dodd, Mead, 1976.

Colman, Penny. *Girls: A History of Growing Up Female in America*. New York: Scholastic, 2000.

Connell, Kate. *They Shall Be Heard*. Austin, Tex.: Raintree Steck-Vaughn, 1993.

Elish, Dan. *Harriet Tubman and the Underground Railroad*. Brookfield, Conn.: Millbrook, 1993.

Freedman, Russell. *Babe Didrikson Zaharias*. New York: Clarion, 1999.

———. *Eleanor Roosevelt, A Life of Discovery*. New York: Clarion, 1993.

Fritz, Jean. *You Want to Vote, Lizzie Stanton?* New York: Putnam, 1995.

Head, Judith. *America's Daughters: 400 Years of American Women*. Los Angeles: Perspective, 1999.

Hull, Mary. *Rosa Parks, Civil Rights Leader*. New York: Chelsea House, 1994.

Jacobs, William Jay. *Mother, Aunt Susan, and Me*. New York: Coward, McCann, & Geohegan, 1979.

Keller, Helen. *The Story of My Life*. New York: Doubleday, 1954 (first published 1903).

McCully, Emily Arnold. *The Ballot Box Battle*. New York: Knopf, 1996.

McLoone-Basta, Margo. *Woman Explorers of the Air*. Mankato, Minn.: Capstone, 2000.

Roberts, Naurice. *Barbara Jordan, the Great Lady from Texas*. Chicago: Children's Press, 1984.

Sherr, Lynn, and Jurate Kazickas. *Susan B. Anthony Slept Here: A Guide to American Women's Landmarks*. New York: Times Books, 1994.

A Few Historic Sites

You can find an internet listing of national women's historic sites at
www.cr.nps.gov/nr/travel/pwwmh/womlist.htm

Adams National Historic Site
135 Adams Street
Quincy, MA 02169

Susan B. Anthony House
17 Madison Street
Rochester, NY 14608

**Eleanor Roosevelt National
Historic Site**
Val-Kill Cottage
4097 Albany Post Road
Hyde Park, NY 12538

Harriet Tubman Home
180 South Street
Auburn, NY 13201

Laura Ingalls Wilder Museum
330 Eighth Street
Walnut Grove, MN 56180

**Women's Rights National
Historic Park**
(includes the home of Elizabeth
Cady Stanton and the Wesleyan
Chapel, site of the Women's
Rights Convention of 1848)
136 Fall Street
Seneca Falls, NY 13148

Some Women's Organizations

Girl Scouts of the U.S.A.
420 Fifth Avenue
New York, NY 10018
www.gsusa.org

Girls Incorporated
30 East 33rd Street
New York, NY 10016
www.girlsinc.org

League of Women Voters of the U.S.
1730 M Street, NW
Washington, DC 20036
www.lwv.org

National Organization for Women
1000 16th Street, NW—Suite 700
Washington, DC 20036-5705
www.now.org

A Note from the Author

If you're going to tell about the women who represent the different chapters in America's story, you must first make a list. Because there are only just so many pages in a book and it mustn't look like a telephone directory, this list of Ladies must have a tantalizing, painful limit: 100.

I set out to be objective, but history's personal. It can't help but be. As soon as I add someone on or cross someone off, it's personal. At this writing, Hillary Rodham Clinton is the first First Lady to run for the U.S. Senate—a bold step for a serious and controversial woman—and yet, if she were in this book, who would not be ? The diplomat? The educator? Or one of the women who turned women's unpaid worlds of conversation and housekeeping into influence and fortune?

Tori Murden rowed a boat all alone, all the way across the Atlantic Ocean. A feat worthy of any history book, but she's not pictured because I'd just finished my paintings. My ship had sailed. It wouldn't have been proper to include my red-haired, beauty-loving mom, who died thinking she was a failure. You couldn't lift the book that told about every woman whose dreams were trampled or folded away.

I invite you to make a list of your own. When you get to 100, you'll have a pretty good idea about your America—and yourself. Mine is a story of 100 players in a pageant about a rich, wild continent of Native Americans, light-living folks, discovered by boatloads of the hopefuls and the hopeless. They and their descendants created a powerful nation based on—if not always lived up to—the ideals of equality and liberty. The people in this book stand for the struggle to make those ideals true for every citizen of the republic—even if that citizen is born a girl.

ELIZABETH CADY STANTON

"The true woman is as yet a dream of the future."

—Elizabeth Cady Stanton
from a speech she gave to the International
Council of Women
in 1888, at the age of 72